WAKEN

THE UNFORGIVEN NIGHT

AWAKENING OUR TRUE POTENTIAL

WRITTEN BY

Raymond Betancourt Jr

COPYRIGHTS

THE UNFORGIVEN NIGHT

AWAKENING OUR TRUE POTENTIAL

CONTENTS

DARKNESS
AWAKENS

DARKNESS
AWAKENS

On October 11, 2020, I awoke early to an unsettling feeling filling my bedroom. I felt a gloom around three in the morning that I hadn't felt in a long time.

This wasn't the first time I had experienced this feeling, but it was just as unsettling as the first time.

As I positioned myself at the center of my bed and tried to make sense of the strange vibrations that seemed to surround the room.

I couldn't shake the feeling of loneliness that washed over me. And then, there were the voices. Screaming voices of unknown people, begging for mercy and asking for forgiveness from a higher power.

DARKNESS
AWAKENS

I could feel their regret and desperation, and it was almost as if I was right there with them, experiencing their pain and suffering.

The room felt heavy with their cries, and I couldn't escape the feeling of darkness that seemed to suffocate me.

Suddenly, my sense of time began to shift. Minutes in the real world felt like years as I was trapped in this dark room, with no control and no light.

I was just a soul, lost in the darkness. This was a night that I would never forget, and one that would burden me for years to come.

DARKNESS
AWAKENS

15. Listen carefully and take heed! Do not be haughty, for the Lord has spoken.

16. Give glory to the Lord your God before it is too late. Recognize him before he brings darkness upon you, causing you to stumble and fall on the darkening mountains. For then, when you seek for light, you will find only terrible darkness and gloom.

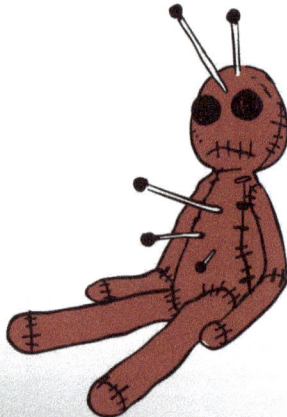

MIRROR
MERCY

MIRROR
MERCY

I noticed something unusual out of the corner of my eye as the screams eventually faded, leaving me once again isolated in the darkness.

The bathroom door was open, and I could see the mirror facing straight towards me, reflecting my own terrified expression back at me. I tried to ignore the open door for what felt like an eternity, but turned out to be a few minutes in reality.

Yet, as the minutes passed, I couldn't get rid of the feeling that something wasn't right. The screams suddenly started up once again. They appeared to be considerably louder and more desperate this time.

MIRROR
MERCY

It was at that moment when I realized that I was no longer in my bedroom. I was trapped in some sort of loop, a hellish cycle of darkness and screams.

As I listened to the individuals begging for forgiveness and mercy, I recognized that I had to get away.

The more I understood about this dreadful darkness, the more aware I became of the absence of forgiveness.

Those trapped within its grasp faced only agreements and suffering. I was stuck there for what felt like a decade, trying everything I could think of to escape and break the cycle.

MIRROR
MERCY

But no matter how hard I tried, I always found myself drawn back to the beginning of this dark and terrifying place.

It was as if I was caught in an unknown dream or universe, unable to escape its grasp.

I was anxious to awaken from this nightmare and return to reality, but every time I thought I had made progress, I would feel a force pulling me back into the darkness. I couldn't shake the feeling of being trapped and alone, with no hope of escape.

This was a hellish experience that seemed to have no end, and I was struggling to survive.

MIRROR
MERCY

God's Sovereign Choice Pride "Romans 9"

17. The scripture states to Pharaoh, I have raised you for this very purpose, to show My power in you, and that My Name might be proclaimed in all the earth.

18. Therefore, God's mercy is extended to those He chooses to extend it to and He hardens the hearts of those He chooses to harden.

THE
UNKNOWN

THE
UNKNOWN

I couldn't take it anymore. The screams and suffering were too much to bear. So I closed my eyes and tried to visualize the source of the suffering.

And as I focused my mind, I was suddenly transported into the experience of one of the unknown people, a man who had been offered the wealth and success he had always dreamed of.

But there was a catch in exchange for all of this, he had agreed to suffer in hell for eternity. And as I lived through his experience, I felt the temptation that he had felt and the weight of his regrets as he realized the true cost of his agreement.

THE
UNKNOWN

In hell, there was no happiness or love. Only poverty and suffering. And this man, trapped in a cycle of regret and misery, was the poorest of them all.

As I witnessed his suffering firsthand, I couldn't help but feel a sense of dread and sadness for him.

The man's regrets served as a cautionary tale, highlighting the dangers of temptation and the need to think carefully before making decisions.

THE
UNKNOWN

9. We are considered unknown, yet are well-known; thought to be dying, yet we continue to live; considered punished, yet not put to death.

10. We are seen as sorrowful, yet always rejoicing; as poor, yet making many wealthy; as having nothing, yet possessing everything.

THE
TRUTH

THE
TRUTH

As I continued to experience the suffering and regrets of the unknown people trapped in the hellish darkness with me, I couldn't shake the feeling that I had to do something to help.

But no matter what I tried, I couldn't escape the cycle of misery that seemed to consume me.

It was only when I connected with the man who had made the fateful agreement for wealth and success that I finally began to comprehend the true nature of my situation.

This man was in complete control of his surroundings and had everything he desired. The deal not only gave him a lavish lifestyle, but it also attracted others to him like a beacon.

THE
TRUTH

But as I stood there and watched him suffer, I realized that the cost of this agreement was much higher than I could have ever imagined. The man was trapped in a hellish cycle of regrets, reliving the moment he had sold his soul over and over again.

It was a powerful and poignant reminder of the dangers of temptation and the importance of making choices with care.

I saw the temptation he had faced and the weight of his regrets, and I realized that I had to find a way out of this hell before it was too late.

THE
TRUTH

I don't know how long I was trapped in that darkness, but it felt like an eternity. But finally, after what seemed like an age, I was able to break free. When I opened my eyes, I was back in my bedroom, and the feeling of darkness and despair had lifted.

It was a strange and unsettling experience, one that I knew I would never forget. But as I lay there in the quiet of my room, I couldn't help but feel grateful for the second chance I had been given.

I knew that I had to make the most of it, and to be more careful about the choices and agreements I made in the future.

THE
TRUTH

Jesus and Nicodemus "John 3"

16. For God loved the world so much that He gave His only begotten Son, so that whoever believes in Him shall not perish but have eternal life.

17. For God did not send His Son into the world to judge and condemn the world, but to save and redeem it through Him.

SPIRUTUAL
REALM

SPIRUTUAL
REALM

The darkness and suffering of that hellish cycle was behind me now, and with a renewed sense of purpose, I vowed to push forward and make the most of the opportunities that lay ahead.

As the end of the year approached, and I looked back on the experience I had just had, I couldn't shake the feeling that I had been given a second chance.

In fact, I started to believe that the only way I could have had such an intense and personal experience of other people's souls and the unknown universe was if I had died and been reborn. It was as if I had been given a glimpse into another realm, one that most people never get to see.

SPIRUTUAL REALM

As I entered the spirituality realm in the years following my experience, I began to understand the true nature of wealth and success.

I saw the difference between the lower vibrations of material wealth and the higher vibrations of spiritual abundance, and I knew that I wanted to focus on the latter.

I was grateful for the second chance I had been given, and I was determined to make the most of it. I knew that I had to be careful about the choices I made and the agreements I entered into, and to always strive for a higher level of understanding and connection with the world around me.

SPIRUTUAL REALM

<u>Walking by the Spirit "Romans 8"</u>

4.   It is through faith in Jesus Christ that the power of the Spirit brings us freedom from the law of sin and death.

5. Those who are driven by their fleshly desires focus on the things of the flesh, but those who are guided by the Spirit focus on the things of the Spirit.

TRUE
NATURE

TRUE
NATURE

I am currently embarking on a journey of self-discovery and inner peace through the practice of meditation.

In my experience, I have learned that the words we speak have a powerful influence on our reality, and it is important to be mindful of the energy we put into our words.

I have personally witnessed the transformative power of manifestation through positive energy and have made a conscious effort to eliminate negative thoughts and emotions from my mind.

This process has allowed me to tap into a sense of inner peace and understanding that I had previously been unable to access.

TRUE
NATURE

I have also come to understand the value of self-awareness and introspection in this journey towards personal growth.

By taking the time to delve deep within myself and understand my thoughts, emotions, and beliefs, I have been able to gain a greater understanding of my true self and my place in the world.

This process of self-exploration has been both challenging and rewarding, and I am committed to continuing on this path of personal development and self-improvement.

TRUE
NATURE

A son values his father's insight "Proverbs 13"

4. One who is able to reign in their speech will live a long and fulfilling life, while those who let their words run wild will find their lives destroyed. 5. The idle desire much and get little, while the diligent are richly rewarded.

Controlling the Tongue "James 3"

6. Of all the body's parts, the tongue is a blazing fire, a corrupting force, capable of contaminating the whole person. It is a world of evil, among the parts of the body, and can defile the entire body and set your whole life on fire, igniting a cycle of greed, envy, and all other forms of evil.

NUMBER
ONE

NUMBER
ONE

It's important to remember that you have control over your body and mind. If you ever feel scared by something supernatural, like a demon or evil spirit, know that they have no power over you.

By practicing meditation and focusing your mind, you can become the master of your own realm. Instead of fearing these experiences, try to take control of the situation and learn to manipulate the environment.

This is what will allow you to manifest your desires in the real world. Through focus and self-awareness, you can achieve anything you set your mind to, just make sure to focus on your desires and not let weakness or disbelief hold you back.

NUMBER
ONE

I wanted to share with others the importance of being in control of our own experiences and understanding the power of our minds.

I had come to realize that my experience in the city where I had my spiritual awakening was unique to me, and that everyone's journey is different. I wanted to remind people that if they found themselves surrounded by negative influences, they should consider changing their environment.

And if they couldn't do that, they should at least try to spend more time outside and away from those negative influences.

NUMBER
ONE

The purpose of my book is to teach others how to awaken themselves and turn their past into something positive.

We live in a cold world where our light is often overshadowed by darkness, but it is up to us, as the chosen ones in our families, to turn that darkness into light.

That means converting negative energy into positive energy, and using that positive energy to manifest our thoughts and desires into reality.

NUMBER
ONE

My number one rule for awakening is "Don't allow negativity in the mind of light".

This means that we should always be mindful of our thoughts and actions, and take the time to review them before putting them into action.

This is what I call self-awareness. And I hope that by reading my book, others will be able to gain the answers they are searching for on their own journey towards enlightenment.

NUMBER
ONE

Jeremiah's Letter to the Exiles "Jeremiah 29"

11. The Lord has a plan for you, it's good and intended for your prosperity, not to bring you pain. He wants to give you a future without any shadows of doubt.

Guard the Deposit "2 Timothy 1"

6. I remind you to awaken the power of God in you, which I passed on to you through my touch. 7. God has given us a spirit of strength, love and self-control, not fear.

TRUE
POTENTIAL

THE EXTENDED VERSION
OF EDUCATION TO WAKEN OUR
TRUE POTENTIAL.

TRUE
POTENTIAL

In this extended version, we will be exploring a collection of rules and principles that can help us live a better, more fulfilling life. These rules have been carefully selected and are based on personal experience and research. They are designed to help us improve our relationships, achieve our goals, and find happiness and fulfillment.

We will briefly introduce the main themes that will be explored throughout the book, including the importance of self-reflection, relationships, and personal growth. We will also discuss the importance of taking action and the impact that small changes can have on our lives to waken our true potential.

CHAPTER 1

EMBRACING MISTAKES

One of the most important lessons that we can learn in life is that making mistakes is a natural and necessary part of the learning process. Whether we are students in a classroom or adults in the workforce, we are constantly presented with new challenges and opportunities to grow. However, as we strive to achieve our goals and aspirations, it is easy to become discouraged and frustrated when we encounter setbacks and failures.

It is important to remember that mistakes are not a reflection of our worth as individuals, but rather a sign that we are pushing ourselves to learn and improve. In fact, some of the most successful and accomplished people in the world attribute much of their success to the lessons they learned from their mistakes.

CHAPTER 1
EMBRACING MISTAKES

In this chapter, we will explore the importance of embracing mistakes and learning from them. We will discuss the different types of mistakes that we may encounter in our lives, and the ways in which we can learn from them. We will also explore the concept of regret and why it is important to let go of regrets in order to move forward.

First and foremost, it is important to understand that mistakes are an inevitable part of the human experience. We all make mistakes, and we all have the potential to learn and grow from them. Whether we are trying to learn a new skill, navigate a difficult relationship, or achieve a professional goal, we will inevitably encounter obstacles and setbacks along the way.

CHAPTER 1

EMBRACING MISTAKES

When we make a mistake, it is easy to become discouraged and feel like we have failed. However, it is important to remember that mistakes are an opportunity to learn and grow.

Instead of dwelling on our mistakes, we should focus on what we can learn from them and how we can use that knowledge to improve in the future.

One of the most important things that you can do when you make a mistake is to take responsibility for it.

CHAPTER 1
EMBRACING MISTAKES

This means acknowledging the mistake, taking ownership of it, and taking steps to make things right.

Taking responsibility for your mistakes shows that you are mature, responsible, and willing to learn from your mistakes.

Another important aspect of learning from your mistakes is to reflect on them. Take the time to think about what you did wrong, why it happened, and what you can do differently in the future.

Reflecting on your mistakes allows you to gain a deeper understanding of the situation and can help you avoid making the same mistake in the future.

CHAPTER 1

EMBRACING MISTAKES

Finally, it is important to let go of regrets. Regrets are the hardest thing to carry when you get older, because they can weigh you down and prevent you from moving forward. When we hold on to regrets, we are essentially holding on to the past, and we are unable to learn from our mistakes and grow as individuals.

In conclusion, mistakes are an inevitable part of the human experience, and it is important to embrace them, learn from them, and let go of regrets. Remember that mistakes are an opportunity to learn and grow, and that we are all capable of achieving great things, even in the face of setbacks and failures.

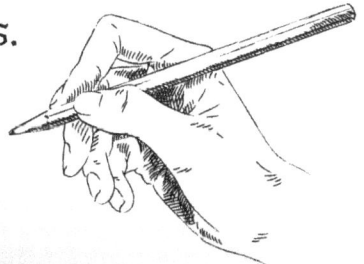

CHAPTER 2
THE IMPORTANCE OF CARING RELATIONSHIPS

One of the most important things that we can learn in life is the importance of caring relationships.

Whether it is a spouse, a parent, a child, a sibling, a friend, or a mentor, we all need people in our lives who care about us and who are there to support us through the good times and the bad.

However, it is easy to take these relationships for granted and to become so caught up in our own lives that we neglect the people who care about us.

In this chapter, we will explore the importance of nurturing caring relationships and the consequences of neglecting them.

CHAPTER 2
THE IMPORTANCE OF CARING RELATIONSHIPS

First and foremost, it is important to understand that caring relationships are essential to our well-being.

They provide us with emotional support, encouragement, and a sense of belonging. When we have people in our lives who care about us, we feel valued, appreciated, and loved.

We may become preoccupied with our own problems, or we may become so focused on achieving our goals that we forget to make time for the people who matter the most to us.

CHAPTER 2

THE IMPORTANCE OF CARING RELATIONSHIPS

When we neglect the people who care about us, we are missing out on some of the most valuable and meaningful experiences that life has to offer.

We are also putting these relationships at risk, as neglect can lead to feelings of resentment, hurt, and betrayal.

It is also important to remember that some people in our lives may not be able to express their care for us in the traditional way.

They may be shy, introverted or have some other reasons that they can't show their affection, but they still care about you. Sometimes you may have to invest time and energy to understand those signs of care.

CHAPTER 2
THE IMPORTANCE OF CARING RELATIONSHIPS

To nurture caring relationships, it is important to make time for the people who matter to us. This means setting aside time to spend with our loved ones, and making sure that we are there for them when they need us.

It also means being a good listener, offering support, and being understanding and compassionate.

Another important aspect of nurturing caring relationships is to be open and honest with the people in our lives.

This means being willing to share our thoughts, feelings, and concerns with others, and being willing to listen to their thoughts, feelings, and concerns in return.

CHAPTER 2
THE IMPORTANCE OF CARING RELATIONSHIPS

Finally, it is important to remember that caring relationships require effort and commitment. They do not just happen by accident; they require time, energy, and dedication to maintain. In conclusion, caring relationships are essential to our well-being and happiness. They provide us with emotional support, encouragement, and a sense of belonging.

Remember that never ignore someone who cares about you because one day you'll realize that you lost your diamond while you were busy collecting stones, and that the effort and commitment that we put into nurturing our caring relationships is what makes them so special and valuable.

CHAPTER 3

FOCUSING ON YOUR OWN JOURNEY

One of the most common pitfalls that many people fall into is the trap of comparing themselves to others.

In today's society, we are constantly bombarded with images and messages of what we should look like, what we should have, and what we should be able to do.

It can be easy to fall into the trap of comparing ourselves to others, and feeling like we are falling short.

In this chapter, we will explore the importance of focusing on our own journey, rather than comparing ourselves to others. We will discuss the negative effects of comparison, and the benefits of embracing our unique selves.

CHAPTER 3
FOCUSING ON YOUR OWN JOURNEY

First and foremost, it is important to understand that everyone's journey is different. We all have different experiences, different challenges, and different opportunities. While we may see others who seem to be more successful, more attractive, or more accomplished than ourselves, we don't know the whole story. It's not fair to compare our behind the scene with someone else's highlight reel.

When we compare ourselves to others, we are usually comparing our worst to their best. We don't know the struggles they have been through, the challenges they have faced, and the sacrifices they have made. Instead of comparing ourselves to others, we should focus on our own journey, and the progress that we are making.

CHAPTER 3
FOCUSING ON YOUR OWN JOURNEY

Another important aspect of focusing on our own journey is to embrace our unique selves. We are all different, and that is what makes us special. Instead of trying to fit into someone else's mold, we should strive to be the best version of ourselves.

It's also important to remember that our journey is not a competition. We don't need to prove ourselves to anyone.

We are on our own journey, and we should focus on our own goals, dreams and aspirations.

Comparison often leads to feelings of inadequacy and low self-esteem. It can also prevent us from taking risks, trying new things, and reaching our full potential.

CHAPTER 3
FOCUSING ON YOUR OWN JOURNEY

Instead of comparing ourselves to others, we should focus on our own journey, and the progress that we are making.

Finally, it is important to remember that focusing on our own journey is not a one-time event, it's a continuous process. It requires time and effort, but it is worth it in the end. In conclusion, Focusing on our own journey is important for our mental and emotional well-being.

Embrace our unique selves, and be the best version of ourselves. And remember that our journey is not a competition, we don't need to prove ourselves to anyone.

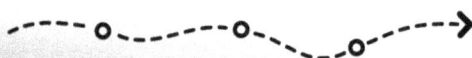

CHAPTER 4

BUILDING A SUPPORTIVE NETWORK

One of the most important things that we can do to improve our lives is to surround ourselves with positive and supportive individuals.

The people we spend time with have a direct impact on our thoughts, emotions, and actions. As the old saying goes,

"You are the average of the five people you spend the most time with."

In this chapter, we will explore the importance of building a supportive network and the impact that it can have on our lives.

We will discuss the different types of individuals that can make up our network, and the ways in which we can identify and cultivate positive relationships.

CHAPTER 4

BUILDING A SUPPORTIVE NETWORK

First and foremost, it is important to understand that the people we spend time with can have a direct impact on who we become.

Our network of friends, family, and colleagues can influence our thoughts, emotions, and actions. If we surround ourselves with positive and supportive individuals, we are more likely to be positive and supportive ourselves.

On the other hand, if we surround ourselves with negative and unsupportive individuals, we are more likely to be negative and unsupportive ourselves.

CHAPTER 4

BUILDING A SUPPORTIVE NETWORK

It is also important to recognize that the people in our network can have a direct impact on our level of success and happiness.

The people we spend time with can serve as role models, mentors, and sources of inspiration. They can also provide us with valuable connections, advice, and support.

When building a supportive network, it is important to focus on quality over quantity, and to be open to new relationships and to be a supportive person yourself.

It is better to have a few close and supportive individuals than a large number of acquaintances.

CHAPTER 4

BUILDING A SUPPORTIVE NETWORK

One way to build a supportive network is to identify the skills, qualities, and characteristics that you would like to have in the people you surround yourself with.

Once you have identified these traits, you can start looking for people who possess them.

This may involve reaching out to people you admire, joining clubs or groups that align with your interests, or attending networking events.

In conclusion, building a supportive network is essential for our well-being and success.

CHAPTER 4

BUILDING A SUPPORTIVE NETWORK

This means being approachable, friendly, and willing to lend a helping hand. It also means being a good listener, offering support, and being understanding and compassionate.

Finally, it is important to remember that building a supportive network is not a one-time event, it's a continuous process. It requires time and effort, but it is worth it in the end.

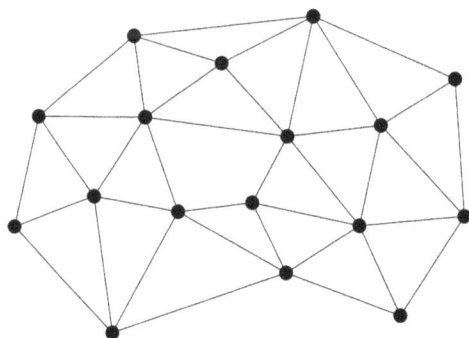

CHAPTER 5

BECOMING A PROVIDER

One of the most important things that we can learn in life is the importance of becoming a provider, rather than just a consumer. The world is constantly changing and the mentality of wealth is shifting.

It is no longer enough to just live paycheck to paycheck and buy the latest products to keep up with the trend.

In this chapter, we will explore the importance of becoming a provider and the impact that it can have on our lives. We will discuss the difference between being a consumer and a provider, and the ways in which we can develop the skills and mindset to become a provider.

CHAPTER 5

BECOMING A PROVIDER

First and foremost, it is important to understand that being a provider means creating value for others. It means identifying a need or a problem in the market and developing a solution to fill that need.

As a provider, you are creating something that is useful and beneficial for others, rather than just consuming what is already available.

Being a provider also means being in control of your financial future. As a provider, you are able to generate your own income, rather than relying on a paycheck from someone else.

This gives you the freedom and flexibility to make your own choices, and to create a life that is meaningful and fulfilling.

CHAPTER 5

BECOMING A PROVIDER

To become a provider, it is important to develop the skills and knowledge that are needed to create value for others. This may involve learning a new skill, gaining new knowledge, or developing a new product or service.

It's also important to change the mentality and habits that are holding you back. This means breaking free from bad habits like living paycheck to paycheck, and adopting a new mindset that is focused on creating value and achieving success.

Another important aspect of becoming a provider is to take action. It's not enough to just have ideas and aspirations, you need to take action to turn them into reality. This means taking risks, making sacrifices, and putting in the hard work to bring your ideas to life.

CHAPTER 5

BECOMING A PROVIDER

Finally, it is important to remember that becoming a provider is not a one-time event, it's a continuous process. It requires time, effort, and a willingness to learn and grow.

In conclusion, becoming a provider is essential for achieving financial freedom and creating a meaningful and fulfilling life.

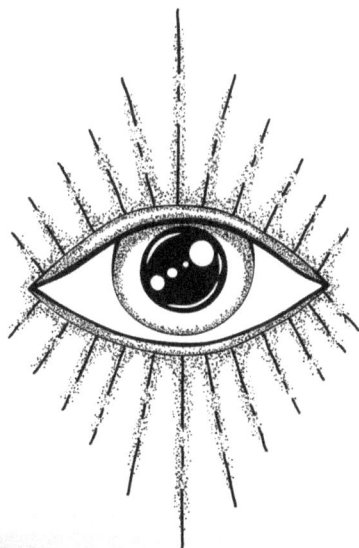

CHAPTER 6

NURTURING THE WHOLE SELF

Caring for ourselves encompasses more than just our physical well-being; it also includes our mental and spiritual health. In this chapter, we will explore the importance of nurturing the whole self and the impact it can have on our lives.

First and foremost, it is crucial to recognize that all aspects of ourselves - mind, body, and spirit - are interconnected.

Neglecting one can affect the balance and well-being of the others. By taking care of ourselves holistically, we can improve our overall health and happiness.

CHAPTER 6

NURTURING THE WHOLE SELF

To nurture the whole self, it is important to be mindful of what we allow into our lives, whether it be the food we eat, the content we consume, or the people we surround ourselves with.

These influences can have a direct impact on our well-being, so it's essential to be selective and surround ourselves with positive and nourishing influences.

It's also important to be aware of our thoughts and habits, as they can have a big impact on our well-being.

Negative thoughts and actions can harm our balance and cause problems such as stress, anxiety, and depression.

CHAPTER 6

NURTURING THE WHOLE SELF

Another important aspect of nurturing the whole self is being conscious of addiction, and taking steps to avoid falling into its trap. Addiction can manifest in many forms and can be difficult to recognize and overcome. By being mindful of our habits, we can take steps to address any addiction that may be present.

In conclusion, nurturing the whole self is essential for our overall well-being. It requires being mindful of what we allow into our lives, being aware of our thoughts and habits, and taking steps to address any addiction that may be present. By taking care of ourselves holistically, we can improve our overall health and happiness.

START
MANIFESTING

MANIFESTING

STEP 1

LIST GOALS TO ACCOMPLISH

YOUR POTENTIAL IS endLESS

✦ ·MANIFEST· ✦

STEP 2

IDENTIFY AND ELIMINATE BAD HABITS THAT HINDER PROGRESS

_____

_____

_____

_____

_____

_____

_____

_____

◇ MANIFEST ◇

STEP 3

REFLECT ON SELF-AWARENESS
LEARNED IN THE PAST YEAR

_____

_____

_____

_____

_____

_____

_____

_____

_____

✦ MANIFEST ✦

STEP 4

ASSESS ACCOMPLISHMENTS AND IDENTIFY AREAS FOR IMPROVEMENT

_____

_____

_____

_____

_____

_____

_____

_____

·✧ MANIFEST ✧·

You got this!

_____

_____

_____

_____

_____

_____

_____

_____

✦ MANIFEST ✦

"The spirituality realm is the path to true wealth and abundance."
- Raymond B.

"The temptation of the material world can lead to eternal emptiness."
- Raymond B.

"The cycle of hell is a reminder of the agreements we make."
- Raymond B.

"Mistakes are opportunities for
growth, not regrets."
- Raymond B.

"Our journey is unique, focus on
becoming the best
version of yourself."
- Raymond B.

"Be a provider, not just a consumer
and you'll have control
over your future."
- Raymond B.

" ———————————————
"Nurture your mind, body and soul, and you'll be amazed at the positive impact it has."
- Raymond B.
"

"

"Don't compare yourself to others, you are on your own path to greatness."
- Raymond B.

"

"Be aware of your habits, they shape
who you are and who
you will become."
- Raymond B.

"Addiction is a trap, be mindful of
what you let into your life."
- Raymond B.

"Be selective with the people you surround yourself with, they will shape your reflection."
- Raymond B.

"You are unique and special, don't waste time trying to be like others."
- Raymond B.

"Don't allow negativity in the mind of light."
- Raymond B.

"Leaving all negativity of the past
behind and awakening
our true potential."
- Raymond B.

ABOUT THE AUTHOR

Raymond Betancourt Jr is the author of "The Unforgiven Night", his debut non-fiction book. He is an entrepreneur and web developer with over a decade of experience in the field. His background in business and technology has allowed him to gain knowledge in various niche areas and continue growing. Raymond believes in the power of manifestation and hard work, and his goal as an author is to educate and inspire others by sharing the knowledge and insights he's gained through his experiences. He hopes to empower readers to reach their full potential and achieve their goals.

54

ACCESS THE SECRETS OF THE UNIVERSE.

TRUE POTENTIAL

WAKENAPPAREL

SPIRITUAL MOVEMENT

WAKENWATCHES

NOTES

Embracing Mistakes

NOTES

Embracing Mistakes

NOTES

The Importance of Caring Relationships

NOTES

The Importance of Ca Relationships

NOTES

Focusing on Your Own Journey

NOTES

Focusing on Your Own
Journey

NOTES

Building a Supportive Network

NOTES

Building a Supportive Network

NOTES

Becoming a Provider

NOTES

Becoming a Provide

NOTES

Nurturing the Whole Self

NOTES

Nurturing the Whole